Living Life With The Glass ½ Full

Naomi Sharp

Copyright © 2014 Naomi Sharp

All rights reserved. This book may not be reproduced in whole or in part without written permission from the author, except by a reviewer who may quote a brief passages in a review; not may any part of this book be reproduced, stored in a retrieval system, or transmitted in any form or by any means, electronic, mechanical, photocopying, recording or other, without written permission from the author.

ISBN-10: 150291350X

ISBN-13: 978-1502913500

DEDICATION

I dedicate this book to all the horses I have met so far and Mother Nature.

Thank you for asking me to be more, and giving me the courage to accept the changes, helping me through stormy days, as well as appreciating all that is amazing and beautiful about life. You have been my constant teacher and I have learnt so much, yet there is still a lot to discover.

CONTENTS

1	Introduction	1
2	Starting at the beginning	Pg 8
3	From mischievous to masterful	Pg 12
4	Through the years the teachers just keep on arriving	Pg 18
5	Venturing to the emerald isle	Pg 29
6	Finding out there is more to life than what we see	Pg 35
7	Seeing the horses in their true role	Pg 39
8	Bonus Feature- creating your own changes	Pg 43
9	Your glass and what fills it	Pg 44
10	Time is very precious	Pg 48
11	Love to learn	Pg 50
12	The seasons of your life, year, month and day	Pg 52
13	Embracing change	Pg 65
14	Saying goodbye	Pg 68
15	If you want your life to change start by changing a day	Pg 73
16	Final thoughts	Pg 81

1 INTRODUCTION

Life is a funny thing, it challenges us every day, and brings us happiness and sadness, sometimes only moments apart. It helps us to be more than we ever expected we could become, yet it can also bring us to our knees.

This began when I was stood in the local butcher's shop and was asked what I do, I explained that I guide people to reach their highest potential. As the conversation progressed I was getting more and more excited about life and the lady chuckled and said "so basically you're an ambassador for life".

Well that set the cogs working overtime as I thought more and more about that statement. For me I would say I am an ambassador for all the things to live for, that makes me tingle every time I think it, and this role has also revolutionised my way of thinking, being and acting.

I have come to realise how precious time is, how incredible our bodies are at functioning, and the perfections of the seasons. I have been through many life lessons that have helped me gain an understanding of the seasons of my own life. When things aren't going right in reality it's probably because they aren't going right in myself, and I have learned not to shy away from this but embrace it and know that I can change it.

Many of us live life thinking we don't have choice, we make them every day and for most people they love to hand over the major decisions to someone else because it's uncomfortable. It's supposed to be, because something old is leaving in order to make room for something new to arrive.

There are many opinions and sources of advice for helping you to live a better and more fulfilled life. But first I believe you need to see how fulfilled you already are, how things are better than they seem. If you blew the worry clouds away you would see that the sun is shining with a blue sky.

So this book isn't here to advise you, or give you tricks to out-manoeuvre your mind - it's here to offer a different perspective and get you thinking to enable you to discover your own conclusions, because as I have said to many people, the only answers that will truly satisfy you are the ones that you come up with yourself.

I have seen life in many forms - the imaginative child, the wisdom of the elderly, the hope of a second chance, or an ending in moments. All our lives are different and we are at different points along the track, but it doesn't mean that we are alone, unloved or lost.

When I was on a transitioning stage from one chapter of my life to the next I used to go on intuition walks.

A bit of background information- I have always been notorious for getting lost. Driving back from the airport I managed to make a trip that should have taken 40 minutes last 3 ½ hours going through 3 counties. I used to ring for help and when they asked what do you see? It would just be a tree or field.

So my intuition walks would consist of me with a back pack full of food. I would head out my door in the morning and walk, muscle testing left or right, or if I saw something that really stood out I would head in that direction. Along the way I would begin to get fearful as I didn't recognise anything around me, but I can say that each time I decided I was ready to head home I made it.

It taught me that there is always a way back to where you feel comfort and safety but also that getting lost or going to new places doesn't have to be stressful or fearful. You can see some incredible sights that you never would have seen, and meet some really interesting people that you probably never would have met.

[If you decide to take one of these walks, please always let someone know you're heading out and in what general direction, and always take some spare clothing and food.]

Talking about going somewhere - where is this book going to take you? The path is yours to take, but I'm adding some sign posts along the way. I hope what you read helps you to make different choices in your everyday life, choices that help you to see and feel that life's glass is truly half full and that things are ok - they may not be what you want but change is on the way.

This book is in two sections-

Part 1 is a handful of my stories with the horses, a snap shot of my journey and life lessons.

Part 2 consists of a few exercises that will help you to create changes in your life and make the transitions smoother.

Who I Am

In the summer of 2010 I was sitting on my living room windowsill looking out over the rooftops of York with the Minster in full view. I was wondering about the possibilities in front of me and asking the question: who am I? This is what came to me:

I am a wild mustang

I need to be handled with care

Be slow on your approach

Let me sense you out, are you a threat?

Touch me gently

Admire my beauty

Take pleasure from life's rhythm

Let me roam, but be loyal and I shall always return

Tend to me each day but don't smother me

Ask, don't tell, otherwise I shall be stubborn and out do you

Abuse me or my trust and I will defend myself

Make a mistake and I will forgive you

Treated right I will be your friend, your companion,

I will help carry your load and take you to your destiny

I will love you and listen to your troubles and keep you safe on your journey

I will keep your days interesting and help you learn something new

I will be by your side in battle

Help make fertile soils for seeds of ideas to grow

I'll work in partnership to keep the herd safe and teach the young
ones the ways of nature

Be my teacher and I will be your guide

I will help you look impressive to others but only we shall know
the secrets

Praise me when I am good but don't punish me when I am bad

Just show me the errors of my ways

When I am scared be my leader

When I am tense help me relax

Be joyful and play in the vastness of Mother Nature with me

Tend to me when I am sick

Leave me to be when I am angry for I will return when I am calm

And most of all love me like I am the only creature who holds the
key to your heart.

The Reason for This Book

Throughout my life I have never been far away from the horse. It has been my ally, companion and most of all, my teacher. I will take you on a journey, my journey to be precise. I have learnt many lessons through different experiences.

A light switched on during the summer of 2010 and I am now seeing what is really around me for the first time. My life has been leading up to this point and what an exciting time it has been. At times I have been on top of a mountain, other times I felt like I was at the bottom of the Grand Canyon wondering how the hell I was going to get out of this one.

There have been many inspirational people who have passed on their wisdom to help me become the person I am today, but there are a few who have stuck around and have helped me to keep moving forward time and time again.

2 STARTING AT THE BEGINNING

I would like to begin by saying that I don't believe in coincidences and that everything happens for a reason. Sometimes it is hard to see the reason straight away, it may be years before the reason for that event reveals itself.

It was announced to those close to the family that I was on the way when my parents and their friends were visiting the city of York on the night of 'Children in Need' (the reason for me telling you this will become clearer later on). When I was born I was the same weight as a bag of sugar, and dolls clothes were the only things I could wear as I had arrived a month early.

We'll start off with a classic story which has been told many times and I thought once more wouldn't hurt. It I went to nursery around 2 years old, it was a little place with only a handful of us as the nursery had only just opened. We had story time, and listening to someone tell a story just didn't cut it for me, so I decided to make it a bit more exciting. Before I go any further I'd like to say that this took stealth, cunning, co-ordination and persistence.

I used to place myself near the back of the group and when the story was in full swing, I would shuffle my little bum to where the toilets were. Then I would get some toilet roll and block the sinks, and turn the taps on, but not too much so they wouldn't make a noise. I would slyly make my way back to the group. I guess you already know what happened next. When the story was over and we went onto the next activity the toilets would already be flooded. This resulted in me being expelled from nursery. After much persuasion and a letter saying "I'm sorry I will not flood the toilets again", thankfully they let me back in.

So I did it again, just to make sure it could be done, of course. Who would have guessed that meant I was expelled for a second time? Then there was the same routine and I was allowed back in. For me, I had achieved all that I wanted to, so the question was how to up the challenge, how about throwing an Inspector in for good measure? So the toilets mysteriously flooded just as the owners were opening the door for the Inspector to come into the nursery. Man, I was in trouble that time. After grovelling and pleading with the nursery, they let me back in for one last time. Have you ever dealt with a horse that kept doing something you didn't want it to do, even when you told it off? It just did it again? Well that was me at this point in my life, until the trouble I would get into outweighed the thrill of doing it.

After the incident with the Inspector, I had proven that the toilets flooded if you turned the taps on and blocked the sinks. This is the point where I stopped, lesson learnt, *always keep my mind occupied, because left to my own devices it's amazing what my curiosity can achieve.* However I was always kept occupied and from then on things went smoothly, and the day that I left there was a comment made by the owners of the nursery "I hope that no one ever breaks her spirit".

For most of my younger years I was dressed in very bright colours as I loved to roam, even when I wasn't meant to, or if I had had enough of doing something, especially clothes shopping (thank you for the invention of internet shopping!) I would sit my bum down on the shop floor and wouldn't move until we were going home. This will be well understood by any horse owners who have had a horse who becomes glued to the spot. The only way you will get them to move is a) making where they're stood uncomfortable or b) FOOD!

The power of food has been my constant weakness and so it was learnt that if they kept me constantly grazing, as they always used to say, a lot more was achieved. So it became a tradition that wherever I went I always had a stash of food in my pocket. Even when walking across the coast line of Cornwall in a full force gale. We were told "it's not much further", three hours later we were still walking. We stopped for a rest and that's when I pulled out the digestive biscuits, the first thing that was said was "where did you get those from?"

This was the time when my riding began. There was a lady who owned a horse in the next village, and she offered to give me riding lessons. I think I was around five at this point. Well that was it hook, line and sinker. I would sit on the horse like a pea on a mountain, so happy walking and trotting round on the lead rein. I can say that the opportunity this lady gave me was a real blessing, and even if I never become some high flying five-star rider, I can say with my hand on my heart that I had the chance to be around one of the most outstanding creatures on this planet.

3 FROM MISCHIEVOUS TO MASTERFUL

As I grew with life experience, my environment started to change as I began to explore further. With it came new lessons that needed to be learnt in order to progress from a child to a teenager. At my first school I learnt about community and friendship. Like most children at that age you are all friends with each other, playing in the school yard. I always used to love break time and especially when they came round with the carton of milk. Each day I would see how slowly I could drink my milk and savour every drop. It was said on several occasions that I needed my own personal cow for the amount of milk I used to get through. I have fond memories of those times, exploring the world, and pushing the boundaries.

Then as the years went by I went to primary school where I

have a vivid memory of the day I upgraded from writing with a pencil to a pen. It was a small transition of learning and mastering a skill, but it gave me a big sense of accomplishment. *This is where I learnt that sometimes it is not the big accomplishments you make in your life that matter, but the small ones that happen every day.*

Then as I began to find my footing, growing and building strength, I wanted to test how far I could push myself, how far can I run? How strong am I against someone else? How can I out-manoeuvre this person?

So naturally I got into sports, I loved anything I could be a part of, as well as the companionship that comes along with participating. I learnt a lot about sportsmanship and *how if you look after everyone around you, communicate effectively and work as a team, nine times out of ten you'll win and be successful.* That was proven when I was part of the football team. We had a great group together and we were heading off to a girls' six-a-side football tournament and as we arrived we were all singing Queen's 'We Will Rock You', knowing that no one at the tournament had an ounce on us. As the day went on, one match after the other, we helped each other. Who wasn't playing was on the side lines cheering, when someone was tired the team would rave them back up, if someone made a mistake another team mate had their back.

The day progressed and we reached the final and talk about suspense! The final whistle blew and it was a draw, down to penalties, the other team scored, then we scored, the other team missed, and it was down to our team member to take the shot. Our team member took the shot and she didn't let us down, we went home triumphant! Looking back *I can see how important it was to have that supportive environment as we all kept pushing ourselves that little bit further with the encouragement of those around us.*

For every high there is a low to keep life in balance. This is when the horse dealt me a valuable lesson. DON'T GET COCKY! I continued to ride outside of school, and as I was getting stronger and more confident it transferred to my riding. We had a horse out on loan that had a field companion which they said I could ride. It was a day in summer and I went down to the yard and fetched in this horse called Minty, which was a small 12hh ish grey pony.

This day is imprinted on my mind. I remember going to the field and trying to catch him, he wasn't having any of it, food was a higher priority than work (which I can totally understand), however, with a bit of help I caught Minty. I took him to the yard and got him tacked up. Now the first lesson: *listen to your intuition!* I had that deep down feeling that something just wasn't quite right, but being only nine, that didn't register as a warning flag. Next lesson: *don't attempt to get on a horse's back if you're not 100% sure.* If something is bothering you, figure it out and resolve it before getting a leg either side of the horse. So I got on the horse ignoring that feeling. *Next lesson: if you don't listen to the lesson that is being taught, it will come back round again and hurt a thousand times more.*

I walked Minty round for a bit and then I asked for trot. I bet you won't have seen a more gymnastic horse with hooves and legs in all directions (well that's how my imagination remembers it). It ended up after the third buck putting me in my place, which happened to be firmly on the ground a few millimetres away from fresh s**t. I had also broken my elbow in the process. I had been firmly placed on the ground and I had tears rolling down my cheeks, trying to figure out what had just happened. I heard the sympathetic words of wisdom "stop crying, get up and head to the house". *Next lesson: don't look for sympathy for your own foolish mistakes.*

I went to the house, got a sling on and was picked up and took to the hospital to get sorted. Now being me that wasn't too bad, I was laughing at my idiocy on the way to the hospital, but then the really traumatic bit of the whole day happened. We went into A&E, got booked in and sat in the waiting room. I was placed right in front of where all the food was sold, I had a clear view of the variety and smells of different foods and those special words that followed have haunted me "you're not allowed to eat anything". Well that was it, I felt like I had just had ten rounds with Mike Tyson. So I got sorted with a cast and headed home.

Six weeks later and lots of milk consumed, my confidence was now scattered to the wind, and it was time to get my bum back in the saddle. So we found a local riding stable where I could take lessons. Here's where the horses taught me their *next lesson: you can't lie to a horse (no matter what excuses you can come up with, just don't do it, you're only lying to yourself).* Honesty is the only way to act around horses. I had gone to the yard and explained about my fall, then started to take lessons. The first few were fine; I toddled along still with confidence at zero. I went for my usual Sunday lesson and when I arrived I went to find my horse. I was about as nervous and shaky as a leaf in a hurricane. Anyway they put me on a horse saying it was quiet, it wouldn't do anything wrong. Well a minute into the ride the horse went down to roll whilst I was on him. That was it - I threw in the towel and said "enough is enough". Thankfully I got off in time before the horse rolled me into a flat pancake.

Looking back on that now I can see that the horses had taught me *another lesson: don't promise something that is out of your control. There is no such thing as an experience where there isn't a risk involved, and if there isn't an element of risk then we will never learn or grow into our full potential.* So I was moving into my teenage years with a fair few lessons learnt, and a few bruises to show for it.

4 THROUGH THE YEARS THE TEACHERS JUST KEEP ON ARRIVING

Well the towel was on the floor for a few months and then I picked it up and tried again.

I began secondary school and started hanging around the horses again. I said earlier how I was like a leaf shaking in a hurricane, well this next memory shows how daft I had got with the horses. I would go down to the yard to help out, until one day it was suggested it was time for me to try riding a horse called Murphy. After being around them again and getting the desire back, I agreed. I got on, and literally within the blink of an eye I was off again with my feet firmly back on the ground, I'm sure I beat all records for the quickest dismount that day. There was a look of confusion from those around, and then came the reason of all reasons for getting off a horse in such a hurry - he neighed.

Yep that's right - he neighed to his stable mate. That sure did create a few laughs! There have been many times since then that laughter has got me through things, however, this noble steed's kindness and caring nature built my confidence back up and there began my lesson of friendship. I guess horse owners who have developed a deep friendship with their horses have that same feeling too.

Just to make a slight detour, sometimes in life I would also get a lesson or two from Mother Nature. Apart from horses, I also love water; I enjoy the power of it, the rhythm of the waves and how on a sunny day the sea sparkles like someone has scattered a thousand diamonds across the surface. The lesson began when my family and I were away on holiday, and we went sailing. We found a boat yard, hired a small sailing boat and headed out to sea. I was in charge of the sails and ropes.

On rare occasions my curiosity serves me well, especially in this instance. I was enjoying being out on the water when I asked "what should I do if the boat starts to capsize?" The reply was "just let go of all the ropes and the boat will stabilise itself" (you can see where this is heading). A few minutes later it was put to the test as a strong wind took hold of the sails and the boat began to capsize, so I did what I was told (which doesn't happen very often) and let go of the ropes and the boat sorted itself out and became balanced. The reason why I tell you this is because this thread of knowledge has kept me safe on numerous occasions.

I transferred this knowledge over to the horses and life *as in certain situations all you can do is let go, let go of trying to control the things that are out of your control.* For me that was a hard one to learn, trusting in something else to keep me safe and get me through a sticky situation, yet it is a lesson that needed to be learnt and I am very thankful to have learnt it, even though sometimes it takes a lot of courage to do.

So from riding Murphy, I also decided to try again with the riding schools. This is where my opportunities really started to open up. The yard I went to became a second home, where over the years I obtained horses by adoption (a type of loan), got a job and over a period of six years worked up to looking after the yard on certain days and when my boss went away.

The horses that I needed for certain times in my life always found their way to me, and so being a stroppy teenager I got a horse called Fudge. She was a 13.2hh dun, and very intelligent. Just by being herself she taught and helped me to become who I am today. She would bite, kick, refuse at jumps any higher than 2ft, and only go when other horses went. So I became more confident and assertive in what I asked, I learnt not to get annoyed when things weren't working out, and I learnt that you have to ride and not just be a passenger. I think the fondest memory I have is going hunting (I know this is a dodgy subject) when it was all legal and above board.

My boss at the riding stables took me and another couple of girls. I was excited as well as absolutely pooing my pants! So we turned up and I got on. As we set off my boss said "just stay behind me and if there are any problems, just put your horse right behind my horse". Fudge hadn't been hunting before, so it was a new experience for both of us. We set off with me holding onto a chunk of mane, following my boss. Then we got to the field where the Huntmaster set off at a steady canter down a field very calm and collected. Well being collected and lady-like wasn't Fudge's style, and neither was it mine.

Staying behind my boss lasted about 30 seconds. Fudge didn't quite understand why she should wait behind this horse when the fun was up front, so she overtook, because at this point I was no longer the leader, I hadn't the foggiest what I was doing, so Fudge stepped up to the mark. What a fantastic job she did, we were going fast but it was manageable. We arrived at the woods and as mentioned before, jumping wasn't really her thing (I thought) but I followed another horse and then we came to a pile of logs. It's one of those things that I wish I had gone back and measured the height of the pile of logs, because anyone who knows about hunting, jumping small isn't really something they do. Anyway the decision had already been made that we were jumping it, and we flew.

The rest of the day went well - jumping up ditches, cantering across fields, a lot of stop-starting. But a good day was had by all. The lesson that Fudge taught me was: *sometimes a bit of tough love is what is needed to bring out your hidden qualities. You also sometimes have to put your trust in someone else to help push past what you thought you were capable of, in order to see that the only limitations on life are the ones you set yourself.*

Being a typical teenager I grew and grew, which meant that I needed roller-skates attached to my feet in order to ride Fudge. So Bob was brought, he was a newcomer to the yard, a 14.2hh cob. He was lovely; his temperament was of a gentleman who wasn't really sure how to be manly. He could turn on six pence when a leaf moved in a hedge! He gave me a good seat though and he had a cracking jump in him.

So we enjoyed show jumping, cross country in the fields, hacking and even a dressage competition. He gave a lot and asked for very little in return (mainly food). He was the horse that I started to apply what I had learnt so far in riding to help him become a better horse and gain more confidence. He taught me: *to apply what you know, because if you don't you won't find out where the gaps are in your knowledge. He also taught me that it takes a lot of hard work to become better at something, but if you master it then you will have it for life.*

I was at the point where I was happy to sit on any horse, just to be able to ride as I didn't have my own horse. So someone offered me a chance to ride a 15hh chestnut mare called DT. I did what I knew at the time and got on, walk, trot and cantered it, and thought I would have a go at a small jump. I started cantering at F, went past A, and set up for the jump, blank, I became aware of where I was at B. I was on the ground with tears rolling down my cheeks, snot all over my face, and winded. I don't know if you have ever been truly winded, but it is a scary place to be, as you are gasping for air but you feel like nothing is going into your lungs. I was thinking "if I don't get air into my lungs soon I'm not going to be around for much longer".

I was mopped up and thankfully regained my breath, and taken down to the yard where I was picked up. I was taken home, given a hug and said "time for a cup of tea". May I just say that the creation of tea is an absolute god send, I don't know of anyone who hasn't gone through something tough or who is celebrating, and the first thing they do is put the kettle on. Like I say I can't remember to this day what happened, the last thing I can remember is turning for the jump. *This lesson: some things are better left unknown or forgotten.* I was told later that I had gone over the jump when she started bucking which began to unseat me and then she took off round the corner. At that point I was out the side door, hit the flood light post, then the fence, before reaching the ground. Back to square one, but this time with a difference. DT left me with a very important question: why did she want me off so badly?

For every fall from grace there is a hero to help pick you back up. Introducing my knight in shining armour: Magic, a 15.3hh piebald. He was as sturdy as a rock; there could be an explosion next to him and I doubt he would have blinked. To most people who saw him move, they would say he was nothing special, heavy footed, not flexible, didn't know he had four legs (I think by the time I finished riding him he knew about three). But for me he was a great friend. He was caring, playful, fun and nothing would budge him.

Have you ever had the experience in your life where you expressed every emotion possible at someone and they just stood there not reacting? Instead they just give you that loving look as if to say "are you finished"? Well that was

Magic. The best memory I have of him is a cracker. We were having a go at Le Trec in the arena, carrying out the activity where you trot between two poles that have been laid down on the floor, parallel to each other, but close enough to just about fit a horse through. We came in trotting (straight lines weren't Magic's strong point, to be able to do a straight line you need to know you have four legs), and as we were going through the poles, Magic put one of his hooves down on a pole, which rolled, resulting in him losing his balance. I was laying on the floor and so was he. I just remember in a split second looking up at him, and catching his eye, and you could just see what he was thinking "OOPS! I wasn't meant to do that!". The memory still makes me laugh today.

He gave me a really good year before he was sold on. So he moved on, and so did I. The lesson he brought to me was: *there are people in the world who, no matter what you do, will just stay focused on your true self as they know that all that emotion isn't the truth. Instead of reacting, they just lovingly carry on and wait until your happiness returns.*

In my late teenage years, going out socialising and drinking lots didn't really float my boat. I'm not one to follow the crowd and drinking excessive amounts all the time doesn't really do it for me (unless there is whisky involved). However, dancing is something I love to do as it is the thing in life where all my barriers are lowered and I am free in that moment. However, I refused point blank to wear pink which ruled out ballet as a child. So, I found a local salsa class, and I took to it like a duck to water. I went to classes and social events where I had a great time, meeting new people and dancing.

With Magic moved on, Rags took his place. Rags was a mare who wasn't in the best condition when we first visited her. We brought her back to the yard and commenced many hours of hair trimming using cow clippers because horse clippers wouldn't go through her fur as it was so long. A duvet could have been made out of all the hair! Rags was sweet, with a heart of gold, and even if she didn't quite understand what I was asking her, she tried with all her might.

At this point in my life, even though I had started salsa and was able to ride Rags, my life was like swimming through rapids. I had struggled with school (I find out why when I get to university), but I had managed to get by. By this time I was sitting my A-Levels and trying to get the grades to be a physiotherapist. However, I fell short, so I turned over the next page in the prospectus and there was an occupational therapy course. I can still remember my grandma saying "I have had one of them, they're good people". So the decision was made - I applied for that course as the entry requirements were lower than for physiotherapy.

But when I came to do my application and get my predicted grades I fell short again by one subject. I pleaded with them to change it to a higher grade so I could go to university. I then gave up my lunchtimes to go to the classroom to do extra studying on the subject. Because to be quite frank I was sick and tired of people telling me that I can't, that I wouldn't be able to, and just because I learn differently I couldn't have the same opportunities as others, I was on a mission to beat the system. So I studied all day changing my subject into pictures, mind maps, tables anything other than word format. So stuff at school was pants, home life brought its own challenges as people around me were dying left, right and centre. There had been double figures of deaths of people who my family knew and a few family members too in less than 12 months. But reflecting back on this time of life I am so thankful for the way it all played out because afterwards *I was no longer afraid of dying, I recognised how precious life is and how precious our time is, and not to take it for granted.* From this point on I vowed to myself *not to waste time, to set goals full of things I want to experience each year, achieve them and enjoy it.* So when I pop my clogs I will not be there thinking "I wish I had done that or regretted saying this", and as a result became incredibly focused on just what I wanted to get out of life.

This is when Rags' heart of gold was a life line, as words could no longer sum up how I was feeling, and there were times when I would just fetch her from the field when no one was on the yard and brush her, until I had brushed away all my sadness. There is nothing big enough to show how thankful I am to my boss and Rags, as I used to saddle up and go out on long rides, with no hesitation and use the yard as a place of safety from life. Rags gave me freedom, I could go anywhere: nothing could block me, I could go along roads and if they stopped I went onto the fields. No one was around for me to pretend, it was just me, the horse and Mother Nature. Yet I was still asking the question: why did DT want me off so bad?

The hardest times in our lives, are the times we grow the most. They are our true blessings. Triumph! Take that education system! I got the grades I needed to be able to go to university, and for the subject where I had asked to get the grades changed, I ended up getting full marks on the exam. People had stopped dying. Out with the old and in with the new.

5 VENTURING TO THE EMERALD ISLE

So I ventured to new lands, actually a new county, to start the next chapter in my life: it just so happened to be York. This was a happy time because I couldn't wait to leave, yet sad too, as it meant leaving the horses and all the comforts of home. I was moving to a city (thankfully a very small one, I'm definitely a country girl) to start my occupational therapy training where I got tested and told I was dyslexic and so gained extra support. I made new friends, whilst keeping in touch with my old friends. I'm not a typical student as my time and effort went into studying instead of drinking, but there were opportunities for dancing. This meant I had a three month stretch with no horses, before I went back home for the holidays and got my horse fix back at the yard.

Then I moved into my second year at university. This is when a friend came to visit me and she told me about working pupils, where you work at a horse yard and in return you get food and accommodation. I had four free months in summer coming up, one month I had agreed to go and look after the yard at home, which left me with three months. So we did some searching on the internet and found a yard in Ireland.

My birth stone is an emerald, and I couldn't think of a better time for the emerald to go back to the emerald isle and maybe answer my question from the horse: why? This is where I met Mozart and Jacob and I learnt what hard work really meant. But I enjoyed every minute of it and the information that I learnt there was invaluable, knowledge that is mainly learnt from being around people who have lived their whole life working with horses. Tips like don't use salt water on a horse's open wound as it dries the skin and the wound will take longer to heal, as well as lime powder on a healing wound means that there will hardly be a scar left.

I have good memories from Ireland, one being me and the girls I was working with going out one evening riding. There was a river just the other side of the field. So I put Mozart's bridle on and we rode to the river bare back. When we got there we rode into the river. I can't describe how it feels to ride in water; it's an experience I shall never forget. The next memory was going into the herd as one of the horses had injured its leg so the owner wanted lime putting on it.

Another girl and I headed up to the herd and caught the horse and I put some lime on its leg.

The herd had over 30 horses in it, and being among all those horses, just socialising, was thrilling and scary as I thought I would be flattened in two seconds flat if something spooked them, but I was honoured to be accepted into the group. *I learnt that it is the people around you that help to change your life.*

Then there was Jacob. He was a very special horse, he had been born and raised in the herd and when I was there he was brought in to the yard a few weeks before I left. Have you ever dealt with a wild horse before? Nope, me neither. But it was an opportunity I couldn't resist. I nicknamed him shaky Jake, as whenever you went near to touch him he used to shake all over. Up to that point I had only sat on horses or lunged them. I have never trained or had the first understanding about how to train horses.

Jacob was in during the day, where I spent every spare moment just being around him, getting him used to humans. Then we went onto lunging him and by the time I left you could clip a lead rope onto his head collar, put a bit in his mouth, put a numnah and roller on him and he could do circles on a lunge line and walk and trot comfortably. I have a lasting memory of him: in the mornings I would bring in the horses that were out in the field, including Jacob, into the shed down a lane. He was a very intelligent horse, and after only a few days of him being part of the routine he not only realised what he was supposed to do but also helped me. I would call at the gate and he would bring the horses to me (they were typically always at the furthest point away). Then he would lead them into the shed and once everyone was in, he would come back out, I would shut the shed door, and he stood by me ready to have his lead rope clipped on and taken to his stable for his breakfast. *He taught me that anything is possible when you know how.*

When this happened I thought, wow, how the hell did that happen? What a clever horse to be able to read my mind and know what I wanted doing. He was another horse that it hurt to walk away from.

Yet I went back to my old yard with a whole new perspective on horses and I couldn't wait to practice what I had learnt, and of course life offered me that opportunity. I was looking after the yard while my boss went away. She had just brought a new horse, and I offered to ride it and exercise it while she was away. This was agreed with apprehension and so it was organised that someone would come and help me with the horse. It was a local horseman who did horsemanship in the area. It went from a new perspective to a new world. The thought that *I didn't have to stay on a horse's back when it was doing movements I didn't enjoy,* was a blessing. Not only that *there were ways to stop that stuff happening while you were on their back, by doing some exercises on the ground,* who would have thought!

It was going good, I had learnt a lot in Ireland and I was learning about the world of horsemanship back in England. Yet I guess my eyes started to wander from the question: why? I went to go and ride the horse and said the famous last words "if I fall off call an ambulance". We rode down to the bottom end of the arena and then he tried to take off, so I did a one rein stop, then when I thought he was relaxed I released his head, and he took off again with a few bunny hops for good measure, so I stopped him again, then we walked on, and it happened again. Now I know anyone who knows something about horses will be screaming at the pages that what I was doing was wrong. The joys of hindsight.

So you guessed it, third time round, I fell off; it was a gentle fall out the side door, only my pride bruised. But the most frustrating thing was I had stopped him twice before and still hadn't sorted the problem out. It left the question like a petrol tank on fire burning inside me: why the hell do I keep falling off? (At this point I can't help but say to myself "well it's because you're not staying on!") , what am I missing? What am I not seeing or doing? And I remember that evening the horseman took me to watch him work on a race horse. I can remember standing there saying "why did the horse want me off so badly?"

So I went back to university, confused more than anything else. But I had my final year of study to concentrate on, which was tough. I enjoyed it though as I was learning about the barriers to participation in adaptive physical activity, as I had chosen it for my research topic which then went on to be published in the British Journal of Occupational Therapy. I then finished university and ended up having my graduation ceremony on the night of 'Children in Need' (21 years to the day it was announced I was on the way). I hadn't a clue what I was going to do next. But in perfect timing my friend was telling me about her experience over the summer at a yard in the south of France and how I must go there. So that's what I did, I emailed the place and asked if they had any working pupil positions and they accepted me. I planned to spend two months in the south of France. But I remember saying before I went "I just don't feel complete, there is something missing inside of me" as I was having another worry rant on what I was going to do with my life, as I didn't want to work in hospitals or the community. My prayers were answered and all was revealed.

6 FINDING OUT THERE IS MORE TO LIFE THAN WHAT WE SEE

In every land there are wise people who know the truth about everything. People go and seek out these people to help them understand the truth. I was very lucky and I didn't have to search far. I arrived at the yard in the south of France and set to work, but was fascinated by how they did everything. It had traits of horsemanship but was somehow different. The amount of research the sisters who owned the yard had put into finding the best way to keep horses was amazing. It is one of those places where, if you spent a lifetime there, you would still not be able to learn everything there is to know.

It was so nice to go back to the very beginning with horses, as they gave me lessons on the lunge; I would have no reins and just ride using my body weight. Anyone who rides I would say have a go at riding on the lunge, let someone else take the responsibility of steering to give you a chance to really understand what riding is about and gain an independent seat. But then came a twist: something that has had a profound effect on my life.

Energy (it isn't as hippy and new age as everyone thinks). It sounds daft I know because we are taught it in schools, and we use it all the time in our lives. This is different but the same, I'll try to explain, but it really comes down to you experiencing it yourself for you to truly understand. It is something more than your mind can comprehend. One of the sisters introduced me to cranial sacral therapy and I was asked to place my hands on a horse's spine and there I felt something moving up and down the spine of the horse, like a ball going from the poll to the dock. After experiencing this I went to watch her carry out a cranial sacral treatment

A lot happened in those 8 weeks, but I will cover some of the key events. I started experimenting with it, because I just couldn't seem to get my head around it. So I would go to a horse (the first ones being Tali and Mojo) put my hands on their spine, close my eyes, empty my mind and that's when I start to feel something.

This brought a whole new slant to riding *if I could quiet my mind enough, I had a better understanding of what was happening in that moment with the horse.* They started to go better for me because I was riding them more positively. It felt like even though I had been around horses my whole life, I had finely tuned in.

There was also an experience that I had whilst riding one of their horses called Kafa. He found it difficult to carry out engagement, which is where the horse uses their ring of muscle and are able to carry themselves in an outline, but the main difference is they are relaxed. Once you see a horse who is engaged you'll realise how many horses are ridden in tension and force. Anyway, I had gotten Kafa to become engaged and then this surge of energy, something I have never experienced before, a power so strong, ran from the base of my spine up and out of the top of my head (some call it Kundalini). After the moment had passed it was like the movements of Kafa had slowed down into little fragments and I could feel each muscle working.

This really opened up my eyes to the possibilities of what riding could really be. I realised how much of the world was untrue, how I had lived my life blind. At this point I realised *there is something called energy, which we can see, feel and heal using it.* Luckily this wasn't something new to the sisters and they supported me, helping me to understand what it was all about. Once you start looking into the subject you'll soon discover for yourself, that there is something to this life that has been too long a taboo subject and once again we are waking up to it.

So I left looking at the world the way I should and how easy it is to create and build a life you want. Knowing what makes me complete and how there is so much to learn, explore and master. I headed back to York and continued exploring the subject.

Which has begun to answer my own question: why? Instead of looking at why the horse wanted me off, *I looked at the fact that it was what I was doing/ being that wasn't working, I just wasn't listening to the horse, as well as seeing and becoming the person I was supposed to be.* The times when I fell off, were the times when I was going off track and *the horses picked me up and put me right back where I should be, as I was so busy with useless thoughts that were hindering my life instead of being present.*

I then spent a couple of months in York looking at life in a new way, researching new areas of health before I decided it was time for another trip.

7 SEEING THE HORSES IN THEIR TRUE ROLE

The degree was completed and the next trip took me all the way to California where I spent three months. The journey began with an 11 hour flight to Los Angeles. Now there is something about being 30,000 feet up in the air (or whatever height a plane flies at) that helps you to gain clarity on your thoughts. During the flight I was pondering on the word disability and its current definition, and then thought about how I would define it, here's the result:

Uniqueness- a person with a disability who poses qualities that are individual to them. A person who has a uniqueness is able to shine their strengths stronger and brighter than someone who is less unique. Yet we are all individuals so we are all unique, which shows there is no difference between abled and disabled, there is only an individual before us. I do not see a child/adult who is disabled with negative traits, I see a child/adult with a uniqueness, I see strength and I see obstacles that can be dissolved in order for the individual to grow emotionally, physically and mentally.

The place I stayed is a charity that takes in the horses that have been rounded up from the wild. Here I got to experience horses on a lot larger scale, as there were around 250 horses on the ranch. The majority of the horses were wild, however, one of the horses was used for the film Spirit.

I loved to go out and sit in the herd, I spent many hours out in the different herds where for the first time I got to experience watching the stallion and lead mare run a herd. I was fascinated by the herd dynamics, how horses interact: from their daily routine to sorting out quarrels. *It was incredible how they said their piece and then it was done, no hard feelings and how simple things were. Also the quarrels and let's say negative experiences were used to teach the younger horses the way to be and interact within the herd and the horses didn't then hold it against the stallion or lead mare, they just understood the lesson and changed.* That was my first experience *that change doesn't need to be complicated, drawn out, it's just uncomfortable for however long you want it to be. If you learn the lesson quickly and change, then comfort and peace are restored.*

I was lucky enough to be there during the foaling time and saw a handful of new born foals just hours old, and one was named Naomi. This is when I saw what I would call true liberty, which is where the foal follows the mum around and it's like watching synchronized dancers. But the fun started as the foal's confidence built, they started to interact with the other horses and became curious. The other horses would play or explain to the foal bluntly that it's food time. The foal made lots of mistakes but that's how they learn.

For me there is too much emphasis on getting it right straight away, I can't think of anything in nature where, when learning something new, they get it right first time. They just keep making mistakes until they get something that's working. So why we expect ourselves to get it right the first time I don't know, it showed me that *to be curious with new things and know that there are probably a whole bunch of mistakes waiting for me but I'll learn a lot from them.* Having this perspective sure does make life look exciting.

My fondest memory was after going up to the herd everyday for about two weeks, I finally got to see the horses at the watering hole. There I watched the horses go into the water to swim, play, roll around or just rest to cool off. I so wanted to go in and join them - they looked like they were having so much fun, it also confirmed in my head that it is a myth that horses don't like water because if left to their own devices it would soon become a part of their daily routine.

My time in the USA gave me the opportunity to explore the diversity of different cultures, meet great people and gain my Reiki qualifications, this is when I began to understand *how much power people have over deciding their own health or using the body's own healing system to improve health*. As well as gaining a deeper understanding that *there are many ways to heal and it is about finding the right one for that individual*, recognising that *the one thing that is consistent in life is change*. Each day every part of life changes: daylight, weather, plants, infrastructure, moods and so on. Absolutely everything is changing yet it seems to be something as humans we resist, when we should really be embracing it. So I said my farewells for now and got on the bus and headed back to LA to catch my flight back to England to start my next chapter, excited to see what it would entail…..

Whilst writing this, I have come to an understanding that *you can see negative experiences as just that: negative and uncomfortable. But that means those experiences will have a limiting effect on your future. But if you see the lessons that are being brought, then you begin to accept the experience and instead of it hindering you it enhances your future.*

Now it's your turn, take a look at the Bonus Feature.

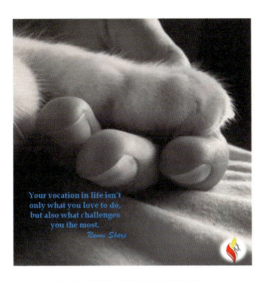

8 BONUS FEATURE
CREATING YOUR OWN CHANGES

This section of the book has not been designed to be read from start to finish. Instead I want you to look at the chapters and when a heading jumps out at you, read that section. Then when you have finished, head back to the list of chapters and pick the next topic.

The reason why I suggest reading it in this way is because you'll be naturally drawn to the information you need right now to help you in your current circumstances. So follow your gut instinct and most of all have fun!

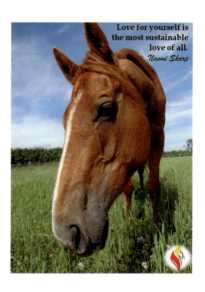

9 YOUR GLASS AND WHAT FILLS IT

There are two ways I explain life to people; the first way is by using the metaphor of a battery. As you move through the day the amount of energy left in your battery decreases, and then at the end of the day you recharge you battery ready for tomorrow. But another way of describing it is by seeing life as a glass full of water and as you interact with people you tip a little bit of the water out. Now for most people they do a lot for others so it doesn't take them long before the glass is empty and people then forget to fill their glass back up by carrying out activities that replenish them.

For me I like to live life with the glass overflowing with water, by having a constant trickle of water into my glass. This means at the end of the day my glass is full or not far off. But I have still spent the day giving to others, instead of using what's in the glass I give the overspill. I get the best of both worlds by being able to give to others, but still having some left over for myself.

First we need to find out what your glass fillers are, as for most people it doesn't take much effort naming what empties their glass. There are two types of glass filler activities: ones that trickle a bit of water into your glass, and super fillers which are like turning the tap on full.

We'll begin with activities which add a little bit of water to your glass. These activities can be carried out on a daily basis, for instance, sitting down for 5 minutes in silence with a cup of tea, reading a book, sitting in the garden and so on.

List 10 activities that make you feel happier and more relaxed once you have carried them out

-
-
-
-
-
-

-
-
-
-

Next are the super fillers. These are activities that you carry out once a month or year which really fill up your glass resulting in tonnes of water spilling over the top, for instance, going on holiday, having a massage, or carrying out an outdoor activity and so on.

List 10 super filler activities

-
-
-
-
-
-
-
-
-
-

This task seems simple but after the third or fourth activity you may begin to scratch your head thinking there is nothing else. It may be there is nothing else that you do currently, but after a bit of research and exploration the rest of the list may consist of things that you would like to incorporate into your life that you feel would help to re-energise and motivate you.

This list is to be kept somewhere handy - on the fridge, in your diary, on your mirror - anywhere that you will see regularly. And when you are feeling rundown or low, pick an activity off the list, then go and enjoy it. Most of all don't feel guilty for doing something for yourself, because like I said earlier, you can't give to others if your glass is empty. So it is in the best interests of those around you if you take time off from your usual roles and top up your glass.

10 TIME IS VERY PRECIOUS

As I write this I have 27,782 days left on this planet (assuming I am going to live until I'm 100 years old).

I so often hear people saying I don't have enough time, I'll do it when I retire, or I'll get round to it. Time is very precious so spend it wisely, those grains of sand are slipping down the hour glass and they can't be gained back.

So don't leave the list of 'Things I'd Love To Do' to the end because you're so busy with the things you feel you need to get done now and saying "I'll get round to it".
Instead, set time each week to:

- ✓ Spend time with those you love

- ✓ Spend time laughing and having fun
- ✓ Spend time leaving a legacy for future generations
- ✓ Spend time sharing stories of your wisdom

If you don't spend time doing this now - when will you? - Tomorrow? Next month? Next year?

I remember the first experience where I learnt the value of time and how precious it is, as well as how we are not in control of when that last grain of sand falls through the hour glass.

I made a promise to myself not to waste my own time but to fill my time with things that make me smile instead. If it's not something worth smiling about like cleaning the toilet, then I use that time to dream about the future full of things that are going to bring more happiness and this leaves me with the feeling of time truly well spent.

11 LOVE TO LEARN

This is definitely an interesting topic and so varied. A trait I see in most people I meet is that they are afraid to learn or try something new because they fear what they have to re-learn in order to accomplish it.

This is where you are different.

My definition of learning is making a whole bunch of mistakes until you reach the outcome you are looking for. It is not a memory game, or test on your vocabulary. It is about being curious about how something works and the results it brings.

This definitely isn't a topic that can be explained in words: this chapter is a practical activity, because to get to a stage of loving learning you need to find something new you want to learn or an activity you would love to do and go and do it! But when things aren't going right, instead of letting your inner chatter say "I can't do this, I'm so stupid", replace it with "I have just learnt another way which doesn't achieve the outcome I'm looking for but let's see if the next attempt brings about the results I want".

One great teacher is 'experience' - we can learn a lot from our experiences and most of us do. This is especially the case if an experience has been uncomfortable - we will then avoid anything that will bring about that result again. It just takes practice to become happy with making a mistake and not letting it discourage you from trying again - it's a great skill to know how not to give up. For me it's not about refusing to give up on an activity, it's about not giving up on myself.

So go out today and make a whole bunch of mistakes and know that you have just found out how not to achieve your goal - which means that's one less way - which brings you one mistake closer to achieving it!

12 THE SEASONS OF YOUR LIFE, YEAR, MONTH AND DAY

The seasons are something we have experienced since we were born. We have all got memories of good times and bad times in each of the seasons. Yet we very often don't recognise what it actually means to our life:

Allowing the spring days to be full of thought and allowing your mind to create seeds of ideas.

Having the energy to keep up with the summer months when you feel like everything is happening at once.

Embracing all the abundance of autumn without feeling guilt.

Handling the stormy wintery days when it feels like nothing is going right.

It isn't very common to think about our lives as seasons and consider what they can do to maximise our lives, instead of just trundling along or going into hibernation. But that's where you're going to gain information and a new perspective on what each day brings. Once you start recognising what kind of day it is panning out to be or what kind of year it is, you will then start to get the most out of life, even the 'rubbish' days actually turn out to be beneficial.

The great thing about the seasons is that I can guarantee in 10 years time there will be the four seasons. Every year without fail the seasons show up - how do I know? Just take a look at nature - even though we may think we haven't had much of a summer, the plants have still grown as much as they could ready for autumn and winter. This is brilliant because it brings some consistency, and with consistency comes security and for a lot of people feeling more secure in life can dispel their worry.

Spring

Spring time in Mother Nature is when the plants and animals are just waking up from their winter sleep and start the preparation for summer. With the arrival of the warmer weather the plants and animals are able to start to replenish their stocks.

But what does springtime look like in our daily lives? It's the times when you get an idea or you are brainstorming and holding think tanks about endless possibilities. It's when you're bursting with enthusiasm for an idea and it's consuming most of your thoughts and you can't help but tell everyone about it because you are so excited.

It's when opportunity presents itself and comes knocking at the door. It's when a chance to experience something arrives, or you find out that it is possible to cross something off your bucket list, or it's an opportunity to meet with someone where you're able to absorb some of their wisdom.

It is definitely a very exciting time full of endless potential, but you also have to be committed. The other seasons are going to follow and this is the time when you decide if you are committed to the idea, if you will nurture it until it grows and you're able to receive the benefits. Are you committed to making the arrangements to go and visit that specific place or person? Are you committed to putting in the hard work of summer in order for it to carry on growing from an acorn into a mighty oak?

So now you can start to recognise when spring is appearing in your life. The seasons don't just happen yearly, they can also happen weekly or even monthly, its less about the time and more about what the time is presenting. Spring may be a Monday morning when you have come up with a brilliant idea on Sunday night and you're starting to bring the idea alive.

But the question is how can you get the most out of spring? First of all - know and accept the signs that are signalling spring. I regularly witness people having the opportunity for a spring day as possibilities are showing up all around, yet they treat it like a winter's day and wonder why things in life aren't moving forward. Once you have recognised it's a spring day, know that now is the time to be really creative and come up with as many ideas and outcomes as possible. Then sit back and choose the ones that you're committed to following through with, the ones that you're prepared to invest some effort in so as to help bring it from a slumber to bursting with life.

Summary of spring

- Ideas
- Opportunities
- Commitment

Then we roll on into summer.

Summer

Most people love the season of summer with its long sunny hot days, BBQs with friends and the kids playing in the paddling pool. Summer is when Mother Nature is in full swing, the fruit trees are flourishing, the grass just keeps on growing, and the plants are soaking up all that extra sunlight and putting it to good use to get the maximum amount of growth in before the fall arrives.

How does summer look in the seasons of life? Growth. You have committed to the idea you had in the spring so now is the time to put in the effort helping it to grow into its full potential. That means that you have to find out what that idea needs in order to grow, what people, resources or environment would help it to flourish. You need to discover what knowledge you need to gain in order to provide the idea with sunlight and water so that it can carry on multiplying.

The efficiency in which Mother Nature is able to multiply fascinates me. If you had a small oak tree which had 3 leaves on it, a few weeks later it would have 6, then 9, then 12 and so on. We need to have that same efficiency when we alter our ideas and lives in order to maintain the balance and which will then allow the idea to keep multiplying and growing.

With all that lovely hot weather don't be surprised if a few thunderstorms show up. Summer is also about gaining strength. This is when your idea has a strong foundation, a solid root system to help it through the thunderstorms. Thunderstorms normally happen when it gets really muggy and the air needs a good clean-up. This is the same with your life or idea. If you suddenly experience a rocky patch which only lasts a day, see it just as a clean-up. Your idea/life was going well but with the new pace, things were getting left unattended, and the thunderstorm just got those bits and pieces sorted out so balance is restored.

Which brings me on to the subject of protecting. Summer is also about protecting what you are creating or living. There are always going to be weeds - the pieces of life or experiences that you don't enjoy will still show up. There is no point putting the blinkers on at this point - it won't get rid of the weeds. You have to put a little effort in and remove them - it's the same with those unwanted things in life - they aren't going to disappear if you turn your back on them. If anything they will only get worse, deal with them, remove them and then you can get back to tending to the flowers of ideas which you enjoy.

If you don't take the time out to attend to the weeds then before you know it you have got more weeds than flowers.

Suddenly the idea or life you were enjoying living is disappearing as it's not able to get what it needs to carry on growing because something else is sapping the goodness instead.

You can get the most out of summer by enjoying the busyness of the idea growing and gathering momentum. Stay organised so that you can make sure that what you are trying to create is receiving everything it needs in order to reach its full potential. Take time to tend to those parts of life that you don't enjoy so they don't end up piling up and then consuming all that you have created. Protect yourself from the negative thoughts or the pessimist, be realistic with what you want to achieve over this one season but don't be afraid to start planning the next summer season because it won't be long before its arrives.

Summary of summer

- Growth
- Gaining strength
- Protecting your idea/ lifestyle

Autumn

I must say autumn is my favourite time of year - the colours are incredible and you receive the rewards for all your hard work. I feel that Mother Nature celebrates the success of the harvest with a firework display of brightly coloured leaves in reds, oranges and browns. But the work isn't done - the animals have to gather the fruit for winter and the plants have to spread their seeds ready for the next spring.

Autumn in our life is just the same. You start receiving the benefits of all the effort that has been put in over summer. For some reason a number of people find it hard to receive through a lack of self worth but mostly because they feel guilty. If you have put the effort in you deserve the rewards! So when you receive something don't have that conversation that goes "oh no I can't", "you shouldn't have", "oh but I haven't got you anything" - just stop!!! Instead say "thank you"; a really simple exchange of words, and not only will you feel better but the person giving will feel better too. A win-win situation. Autumn is about enjoying the fruits of your labour.

It is also about seeing what your efforts have yielded. Like I mentioned before, everyone loves summer but sometimes people want summer to last forever. They hold off on the arrival of autumn. This is not wise - you need to take stock of what you have achieved from all that you sowed back in spring. If you sowed one seed and expected a field full of corn, and were shocked at harvest time that you only got one piece of corn, you know your perception of reality is out of kilter. So have a look at what your harvest has brought - is it as much as you wanted? Is it above and beyond what you thought was capable? Is this really the outcome you wanted? If you can answer these questions you will start to have some ideas of possible alterations that you can make next spring.

So autumn can either be a time of rejoicing or a time of regret, depending on how you spent your spring and summer. If it is a time of rejoicing shout it from the roof tops! Share it with others - what your idea has brought or the life you've built is a great accomplishment. If it is a time of regret then don't shy away from your mistakes, just make sure you change how you carry out the next spring, and see if that yields better results.

Ensure you get the most out of autumn by receiving the rewards of your hard work not with resistance but with gratitude. Make sure you look at what your hard work has created and see where it has flourished above what you imagined or maybe didn't flourish so well because of too many weeds. And don't be shy about your achievements because what you achieve may inspire others to do the same.

Summary of autumn

- Receive your abundance

- Take stock of your yield
- Rejoice or regret, know that it's because of your efforts in the previous seasons

Winter

Then we move into the deep dark depths of winter. Yet people forget the fun winter can bring - the rain and cold aren't appealing but they have their purpose too. You can't beat watching the first snowflakes begin to fall, eyeing up the sledge, wondering if tomorrow is the day?

Mother Nature uses winter as a time of rest, it's been a busy year, and it's time to recuperate, and the frost kills off any unwanted bugs that have arrived in summer. It may be a long winter with heavy rain or snow lasting months or it can make only a brief appearance.

The same goes for the winter season in your life. It may be long or tough going and take its toll or it may just be a fleeting experience, either way it is still as important as spring, summer and autumn.

Winter is a great revealer of someone who is prepared or unprepared. I like to think of it in the following way: someone collects wood and chops it up over summer and autumn to fill up their log store so it's overflowing, ready to be able to heat their home and cook food on over the winter months. On the other hand, there is someone who has spent all their time playing and no time preparing. The first snow fall arrives and they realise they don't have enough wood to last a day. The first person will just need to step outside, fill up the basket and head back into a warm home; the second person will have to spend hours out in the cold, trying to scrap together the few pieces of wood laying around that aren't already covered in snow, going home and having to ration the wood so it can last all winter. The winter months in life are going to arrive and no one else but you can put that little bit aside so you're prepared for whatever life brings. Winter may be your idea not having the same momentum or the pace starting to slow down because you have received a few setbacks.

The winter season in life can also bring despair, loneliness, disappointment or tragedy. I'm sure all people have a story to tell about times like these. They are a part of winter, because even though the times you're going through feel and look bleak, they also have a knack of motivating you. I have met people who share their worst times and then what follows is incredible, they go onto how they committed to themselves that they will learn what's needed or where to go in order to never live like this again. Or they get the courage to leave and never be treated like that again. From these times, a courage and strength so strong emerges that carries them out of the darkest hour and into a new dawn. However, I do appreciate that this isn't the case for some people as they feel helpless as they move further down the spiral - in those cases I would say go and find someone to talk to, the mere sharing of what you're feeling will bring about relief that will begin to help you move up the spiral again.

The last aspect winter brings is rest, evaluation and education. Take the time to rest and recuperate, because spring won't be far away and you'll need bucket loads of energy for summer. Winter is about taking the time to do the things that fill your glass so it's not only ½ full, but overflowing. Let yourself look back over the seasons and recognise the areas that have brought you happiness, the stormy days you got through, and memories of summer evenings. See if the seasons have been all that you would have hoped they'd be, and maybe more. Contemplate where the next cycle of seasons will take you, the things that they could bring. With the long hours of darkness don't forget to get out the books that are packed with wisdom and take the opportunity to absorb, replenish and learn the information which could then be brought to the next spring.

Summary of winter

- Being prepared or unprepared
- Despair, loneliness, disappointment or tragedy can be the darkest hour before a new dawn
- Take the time to rest, evaluate, and educate

Today think about what season you are in and how you can get the most out of it. Ask yourself - are you prepared for the next winter? And ready to receive in the autumn? But most of all enjoy what each season brings and the consistency of knowing that it's all going to start again, with the opportunity try again with the next cycle of seasons.

13 EMBRACING CHANGE

Change happens every day, most of the time without us even realising it. We feel comfort if the changes are small as we find them easy to adapt to. It's when the changes are a bit bigger and may interrupt our daily routine which we find uncomfortable and sometimes even intolerable. Why is this?

Our emotions and imagination

We all have a fantastic imagination and most of the time our imagination is working against us and not with us. This is until we start to be aware of what our day dreams/worries are creating and make an effort to redesign them. It's not the actual change that bothers us - it is what the change may possibly bring. When we don't have control over our imaginations we normally start to highlight all the bad things that will come into our lives now that change has occurred instead of seeing what good it can also bring.

There are two types of changes. Deliberate change is where you are choosing to create space in your life for change to occur and even helping change to arrive sooner. This is welcomed change as you have control of what and how it affects your life. Then there is the second type, spontaneous or unplanned change. This normally sends us into a whirlwind of panic as it disrupts our daily habits, asks us to change our beliefs and values and puts us in a place that we didn't know existed.

Deliberate change can be really enjoyable - using vision boards, setting goals, changing environments - it's a really creative fun time. But we also need to be aware that spontaneous change occurs and we need to be prepared. Here are a few tips to help when spontaneous change occurs:

- ❖ Have an activity ready that will help to calm you down (eg have a cup of tea), when you first hear the news of the arrival of spontaneous change. When you're emotional it will be harder to make logical decisions.
- ❖ Brainstorm all possibilities and their results; most of us lose the fact that there is choice at this point, thinking all choices have been taken away. They

haven't been taken away - they have just transformed into something else.

❖ Have a sound board, have a person who is your back up, who doesn't get rattled very easily and won't make your story into a big drama, explain the change that has arrived and your ideas. Talking it through will help you to feel like you're gaining control.

At this point, even though you may not be feeling delighted about what has just occurred, you will be feeling like you can get through this and normality will return even if things may be different.

For me the fire drill for change is to be aware of all the changes that happen daily, weekly, monthly and yearly so you get used to the concept of change. Then be a deliberate creator by implementing your own changes in life. You'll find that the more changes you implement, the fewer changes other people will implement for you.

Most of all know that change happens, good and bad, the only thing you have to do is keep your imagination from creating scenarios of changes that will feel like they're destroying your life. Instead be optimistic and look for the rainbow amongst the storm.

14 SAYING GOODBYE

Saying goodbye is never easy, and it can leave a lasting scar for most people. The death of a person or animal can take a long time to get over and some people may never get over it. But death also comes in different forms, the completion of a project that has consumed all the hours of your day, or the moving from an environment like your home to a new place. It's that sense of loss, even if there is something better waiting for you. It's saying goodbye to someone or something that has contributed to your life and that has been a part of creating many memories. But does it have to be a sad time that lasts forever? Are there not some parts that can be celebrated?

The void and the unknown

What most people struggle with is the void that is created

with the absence of what has just been lost. There is a space created that you're scared to fill as you don't want to lose all memories of what once was. There is also the fear of what is to come: a void has been created and you don't know what is going to come and take its place, indeed, if anything at all is going to come and take its place. It's like looking into a black hole and wondering where you will end up if you go into it.

But losing someone or something doesn't mean you have lost all of your choices. Even though you're probably not feeling your strongest, you do still have a choice on what takes the place of that void. However, whatever is taking the place of what was lost isn't replacing it or deleting it from your memories or life. I am a true believer that things can never be destroyed but can only transform. So there is no need to feel guilty if you fill the void with something that brings you happiness. I bet if the person or animal could speak from the other side they wouldn't be angry or say that you should still be feeling sad. I'm sure they would say "great – you're ready for this next chapter and the lessons it's going to bring, and I am so happy to see you smile again".

In terms of the void with projects and environments, it's ok to feel sad about their end too, but this is where goal setting is needed to help keep you moving forward instead of getting lost in the abyss. An example is a sports person who lives and breathes a gold medal at the Olympics and who spends their whole life trying to achieve it. But when they do achieve it what else have they got to live for? This is where you need to know what you're going to aim for after you have reached the current goal to stop you spiralling down into sad thoughts.

Putting on a brave face

First of all, it's ok to be sad, upset, scared - let yourself feel these emotions when the day arrives and loss has become part of your story. There seem to be two reactions: melt down or brave face. For me when someone goes into melt down I think 'thank goodness they're not keeping that emotion locked inside'. When someone puts on a brave face my thoughts are 'still waters run deep'. But like with everything there is balance and I don't know anyone who can stay balanced 100% of the time. For me, maintaining balance within is like balancing a broom on the palm of your hand, you have to keep making tiny adjustments to stop it falling off and hitting the ground. It's the same with grieving - you just need to let the emotions be - but don't let them consume you and your life. It's best to let the tears flow then say "ok, time to do one activity today". Then the next day you may wake up and the tears begin to flow then you say "ok let's do two activities today", and keep building your life back up by increasing the amount of activities that you do in a day, until you reach a stage where you have got your routine back. What is the time frame for this? There is no specific time frame; people grieve at different paces but I would speak to someone if you're still not able to do a couple of activities a day and it's a decade after the loss. That would show that you have got stuck along the way of the grieving process.

The grieving cycle

I only want to touch on this, as there is a ton of literature already out there, but there is a sequence of emotions that normally happens when loss has appeared in your life.

- ➢ Numbness
- ➢ Yearning
- ➢ Outbursts of strong emotions
- ➢ Sadness
- ➢ Letting go

Like I said earlier on, these things shouldn't hang around forever, at some point your life will be carrying on but in a new direction.

Celebrating what was and what's yet to be

Ever the optimist, you also have a choice in the memories and thoughts you have on the loss. You can either choose

The absence, void, loss

Or

The memories of great times together, and overcoming obstacles. The lessons learnt that you can take to the next chapter of your life, and the laughter along the way.

I know which side of the coin I prefer to look at. You'll also find that people around you will choose one side or the other. Don't be cross if they choose a different side to you, because that is how they handle loss. But I would always suggest sharing stories of the good times because when you recall those memories the tears turn from tears of sadness to tears of laughter.

15 IF YOU WANT YOUR LIFE TO CHANGE START BY CHANGING A DAY

Everybody's routine is different. My realisation of how important our daily routine is was profound to say the least, all thanks to the clues life had left me along the way.

Now it is not that this is something new, I am not trying to reinvent the wheel, however I think it is something that is extremely overlooked and it is so simple! It is the woven fibres of our day, week, month, year and lifetime and we don't generally give it a second thought.

We all have the ability to dramatically change our life and circumstances, and I spent many years trying to understand this by listening to peoples' stories of how they turned their business, finances or relationships around so quickly. I hadn't taken into account their change of routine.

This book is here to help you to make those dramatic changes and most of all quickly! Once I had understood this little golden nugget of information my life went from good to incredible. I want to share that information with you, so you have the same chance of having an incredible life, the life you deserve.

What is your routine?

To move forward we first need to know where we are at, and most of all not to be ashamed of it. The activities that you are currently carrying out each day are providing you with the results you are getting, it doesn't mean it's where you need to stay.

So let's take a peek; how do you spend each waking hour?

Create a table with the days of the week along the top and the hours of the day down the side. The key is to fill it in with the activities you carry out during a typical week and block off the time spent doing that activity in the table. If you want to be extra snazzy, colour code the activities (for instance sleep, exercise, eating, work, socialising etc).

So now we have a snapshot of your current life: these results may be making you happy, making you want to achieve a new goal or they may be making you miserable.

The good news is that you can carry on doing the activities that are making you happy, replace the ones that are making you unhappy and achieve the New Year's resolutions that have been left on the back burner.

What do you want to achieve

Before heading onto creating a new routine, we first need to decide where we are going. There is a great story that I use to illustrate the importance of a target/goal.

A man was laying bricks one day and a neighbour walked by and asked what he was building. The man replied "I don't know".

Planning your future, by looking at what or where you would like to be by the end of this year, 5 years time and 10 years time, is like drawing up the plans for your life, and then each year making it a reality by laying the foundations and adding the bricks. Even though events can change your plan, it's still handy to have an idea of what kind of life you are trying to build.

Now this is the point where the common phrase crops up: "I don't know what I want". Well this is the time to decide and the most exciting part of all is that you can create whatever you can imagine. This is when you dream big even though it may seem unrealistic right now but you'll be surprised at how quickly things shape up.

So let's get dreaming.

Who/where do you want to be by the end of this year? Be specific with all areas of your life:
Work/career
Relationships
Socialising
Financial
Health
Add to the list any more areas you want to create.

Next, who/where do you want to be by the end of 5 years? Use the same areas as above.

And finally, who/where do you want to be by the end of 10 years?

Brilliant, now you should be feeling good, even excited, as

your imagination is on overdrive thinking about your brilliant future. This is how it should be, it should be exciting, not fearful. Worry is just your imagination creating 'what ifs'. Some golden advice: put your imagination to work on things that make you feel good and excited and not about what worries and frightens you. This is where we move onto making it all possible.

How to build a new routine

This is a gradual process. For it to be sustainable we need to make small alterations. If a plane was flying and it was one degree out of alignment of its flight path when it set off, after flying for a few hours it would be 20 degrees off and would end up in a new destination. If you have ever been in turbulence and the plane suddenly drops in altitude, the adrenaline starts pumping and we become fearful - we try to go back to what's comfortable and maybe even try to avoid the experience. The same result can happen when you make sudden changes that you're not ready for.

Firstly, write the following sentence down on a piece of paper and put it somewhere you look several times a day:

YOUR LIFE WILL CHANGE WHEN YOU CHANGE SOMETHING YOU DO DAILY. THE SECRET OF YOUR SUCCESS IS FOUND IN YOUR DAILY ROUTINE.

On another piece of paper write that saying down as a title on the top of a page and then underneath write down week commencing Monday .... /...../....

Monday .... /...../....

Monday .... /...../....

Monday .... /...../....

Monday .... /...../....

Monday .... /...../....

You are now set up for six changes to your routine, one each week. If you have six ideas of new activities you want to incorporate then write them down at the bottom of the page and pick one for the first week. Hold off on filling in the rest of the weeks until the date arrives. The reason for this is that by the end of the week you will have started to become a new person and after a few weeks the person you predicted you would be and the person you actually are will be different, as you accelerate past what you thought was achievable.

So you commit to carrying out a new activity every week. By

the end of week one that new activity, if done daily, will be well on its way to being a habit, ready for you to concentrate on bringing in another new activity.

How to maintain your new routine

The day of contrast will come, but it doesn't have to stop you. We have stormy days and most of us hide under the duvet until the sun comes back out. You will have days that you will feel overwhelmed, even lost, as your self perception is changing. You just need to remember in those times that storms don't last forever. Only a day, maybe two, but the sunshine always returns.

Build yourself a close network of friends, maybe you will change your routine together and help each other through the process; offer support and guidance in the low times and celebrate in the good times. You might even want to create certificates and present them at the end of each week to those who have done their activity every day.

If you're more of a person who does things by themselves - have something you could go to, listen to a piece of music or watch a video clip that cheers you up and reward yourself when you have achieved your new activity daily.

Lastly, keep your goals handy so you can keep an eye on the life you are building, and don't be afraid to change things if you have gone above and beyond what you thought was possible at the start.

Ever evolving routine

At the end of the six weeks re-evaluate to see where you are at, are you on target to reaching your goals? Are the goals still applicable or have you refined what you want to do? Do you want to set bigger changes? Were the first six weeks just a trial - and you like the improvements - so now want to do another six week block?

As you progress through your life and keep achieving your goals you will have to keep evolving your routine. Now, human beings are brilliant creatures of habit and we really avoid having to change our routine, but that's where your desire to achieve your goals drives you to make those changes.

Also keep a record of all the changes you have made successfully and those which were unsuccessful with the reason why. It's not a problem if one is unsuccessful, it just means it wasn't quite in line with what you were trying to achieve or it was too much of a stretch. You can continually refer back to your notes and see all that has changed for the better. This can also be a source of motivation on the contrast days.

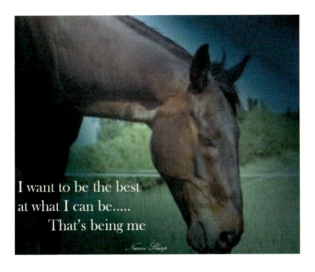

16 FINAL THOUGHTS

To round up I would first like to share with you my own definitions of four key words, which I think run strong throughout all our lives, these are:

Hope

Hope is to wish for and welcome something, with the expectation of its fulfillment with confidence and belief. It is to desire something, with little reason or justification, by cherishing and trusting in the aspiration of good.

Destiny

Destiny is an event that will inevitably happen. However,

any individual with the power of thought can make choices which may affect their own future by taking considered actions that define and influence the eventual outcome.

Fear

Fear is to suspect and doubt. To experience feelings of fright, concern and agitation, but gain the feeling of profound respect for someone or something, with awe. To feel fear within (oneself) is to be able to drive away or prevent the approach of apprehension.

Beauty

Beauty is the quality that gives pleasure to moral senses, with grace, excellence and truthfulness. It is to have the confidence to be outstanding and original.

After all life has taught me so far, the best way to sum up my final thoughts is through sharing with you my own personal principles on life:

- Always plan your year but be flexible in allowing it to go above and beyond your initial idea.
- Self love is the most sustainable love of all.

Living Life With The Glass ½ Full

- Live to learn, take each day's experiences and learn from them; experience is our greatest teacher.

- Your vocation isn't only what you love to do but also challenges you the most like a top athlete.

- Anything is accomplishable if you're prepared and organised.

- Start your bucket list this year, not in your last year.

- Clutter is unfinished projects; finish the projects and the clutter will disappear.

- Learn to read your own signposts.

- Nature and animals are a gift to bask in, take time daily to do so.

- Storms in your life will always occur, they may leave devastation in their wake, use them as an opportunity to build something better.

- Be aware of your values and beliefs, allow them to evolve.

- Never complain about getting old: it's a privilege not everyone gets to have.

- Lead by example: you'll have more people following.

- Find your way to quieten worry and allow change.

- Your environment is a key motivator, invest in it and make sure it's how you want it. Don't settle for anything less.

- Trust your gut instinct when making a decision and follow your intuition.
- Dance daily: movement cleanses the mind, body and soul.
- To release resistance change the direction you're going.
- If you want to change your life start by changing a day.
- Enjoy each season and what it provides.
- Death is inevitable but it's your choice how much fun you have leading up to it.
- Time is precious: don't waste it on negative thinking.
- The only clock you have to follow is day & night.
- Anyone can become anything even if it's only in their imagination.
- The best thing you can be is yourself.
- Make sure your image reflects you're goodness.
- Don't wait until you die to celebrate your great life.
- Be optimistic, life's a lot more fun and things are achieved more quickly.

Have a safe and happy journey through life ☺

ABOUT THE AUTHOR

Naomi Sharp trained as an Occupational Therapist but became fascinated in how horses help people to heal not only physically but also mentally and emotionally. Her passion for understanding how we can help our bodies to heal and our dreams to become reality has brought some breath taking experiences into her life. As well as the opportunity to meet some incredible people and places.

www.spiritofthephoenix.co.uk

Printed in Great Britain
by Amazon.co.uk, Ltd.,
Marston Gate.